Newbridge Discovery Links®

EYE ON THE UNIVERSE

Sean Price

Newbridge

A Haights Cross Communications Company

Eye on the Universe
ISBN: 1-58273-735-5

Program Author: Dr. Brenda Parkes
Content Reviewer: Dr. Charles T. Liu, Astrophysicist, Department of Astrophysics,
  American Museum of Natural History, New York, NY
Teacher Reviewer: Lisa Donmoyer, Talbot County Schools, Easton, MD

Written by Sean Price
Editorial and Design Assistance by Curriculum Concepts

Newbridge Educational Publishing
333 East 38th Street, New York, NY 10016
www.newbridgeonline.com

Cover Photograph: Photograph of nebula, taken by Hubble
Table of Contents Photograph: Hubble in orbit above Earth

Photo Credits
Unless otherwise noted below, all photographs are courtesy of NASA.
page 5: (bottom) The Granger Collection; page 6: (left) Bettmann/CORBIS, (right) Hulton-Deutsch
Collection/CORBIS; page 7: Bettmann/CORBIS; page 8: Courtesy of the Naval Research Laboratory;
page 9: (top and bottom) Roger Ressmeyer/CORBIS; page 18: CORBIS; page 25: (top) STScl/NASA/
ASU/Hester/Ressmeyer/CORBIS; page 26: (top) NASA/Roger Ressmeyer/CORBIS; page 27: (center)
CORBIS

Illustration by Steve Stankiewicz, page 11

TABLE OF CONTENTS

Have you ever wanted to look back in time? Believe it or not, you do just that every time you look at the nighttime sky. Many of the stars up above are several **million trillion** miles away. Light travels through the **universe** at 186,282 miles per second. Nothing in the universe travels faster than light. But even at that speed, the light from some stars still takes billions of years to reach us.

The Hubble Space Telescope was designed to be one of the greatest time machines ever. Orbiting about 370 miles above Earth, it can peer deeper into space—and farther back in time—than most other telescopes. Its remarkable story actually began in 1608, when a Dutch optician named Hans Lippershey invented the very first telescope. Not long after, Italian **astronomer** Galileo Galilei adapted and improved Lippershey's device.

★ ★ ★ ★

The 25,000-pound Hubble Space Telescope (far left) is as big as a school bus. Galileo (left) used the first astronomical telescope to show that Earth moves in an oval around the sun.

The telescope Galileo used was a simple tube with two glass lenses that refracted, or bent, light. The **refracting telescope** used one large lens (called an objective lens) to collect light, and another smaller lens (called an eyepiece) to magnify the picture. Then in 1668, English scientist Sir Isaac Newton created one of the first **reflecting telescopes**. In this new kind of telescope, the light went into a tube and reflected, or bounced, off the mirrors and into an eyepiece.

Newton's reflecting telescope gave a clearer picture than Galileo's, so it became more popular with astronomers. Over the centuries, scientists made their telescopes larger and larger to collect more light and, therefore, see farther. This allowed them to do trailblazing work. For instance, Annie Jump Cannon systematically classified thousands of stars in the late 1890s and early 1900s.

★ ★ ★ ★

In the 1600s, Sir Isaac Newton (left) built a reflecting telescope that helped him form important theories about how the universe works. American astronomer Annie Jump Cannon (right) classified 350,000 stars.

★ ★ ★ ★

The Hubble Space Telescope was named after astronomer Edwin Hubble, shown here at California's Mount Palomar Observatory.

The work of Edwin Hubble was also of great importance. In the 1920s, Dr. Hubble discovered that our **galaxy**, the Milky Way, is just one of many in the universe. He also showed that the universe is expanding.

Scientists still had many questions. For instance, what's the shape of the universe? How do planets, stars, and galaxies evolve? And how many galaxies are there? The Hubble Space Telescope was created to help answer those and other important questions.

Hubble could help scientists answer such questions because it orbits above Earth's **atmosphere**—the blanket of gases surrounding our planet. Even on clear nights, those gases block and distort light from the stars. In fact, it is the atmosphere that causes stars to appear as if they are twinkling.

As early as the 1920s, scientists had dreamed of placing a telescope in orbit above the atmosphere. Such a telescope would be able to see images ten times sharper than the biggest telescope on the ground. It would also see different types of light—like **ultraviolet light**—that are blocked out by Earth's atmosphere. After years of study by astronomers, the U.S. Congress approved funding in 1977. The Hubble Space Telescope was about to be born.

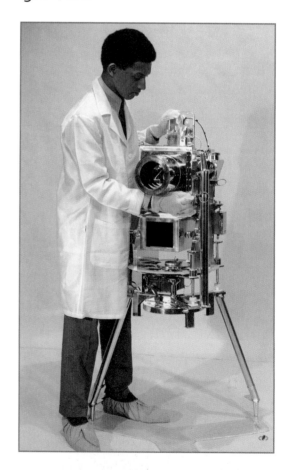

Astrophysicist George Carruthers pioneered a space camera that picks up ultraviolet light. Carruthers is an adviser to the Hubble program.

★ ★ ★ ★

Giant observatories like the W. M. Keck Observatory in Hawaii are often put on high mountains where the atmosphere is very still. The photograph above shows the inside of Keck.

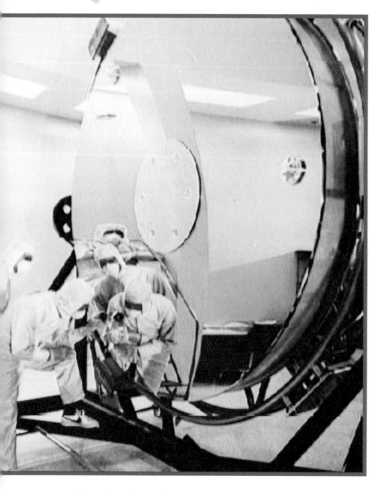

Hubble's primary mirror is shaped like a shallow bowl and weighs about 1,800 pounds.

Many telescopes besides Hubble have been sent into space. But so far, Hubble is the largest, and therefore has the keenest eye. Hubble is a modified version of Newton's reflecting telescope. At its heart is a system of mirrors that reflect light into several cameras and instruments. The largest of those mirrors is the primary mirror, which has a diameter of about two meters.

While Hubble was being built in the 1980s, engineers knew the primary mirror had to be ground exactly right. It had to be curved perfectly so that it focused light into a clear image.

THE HUBBLE TELESCOPE

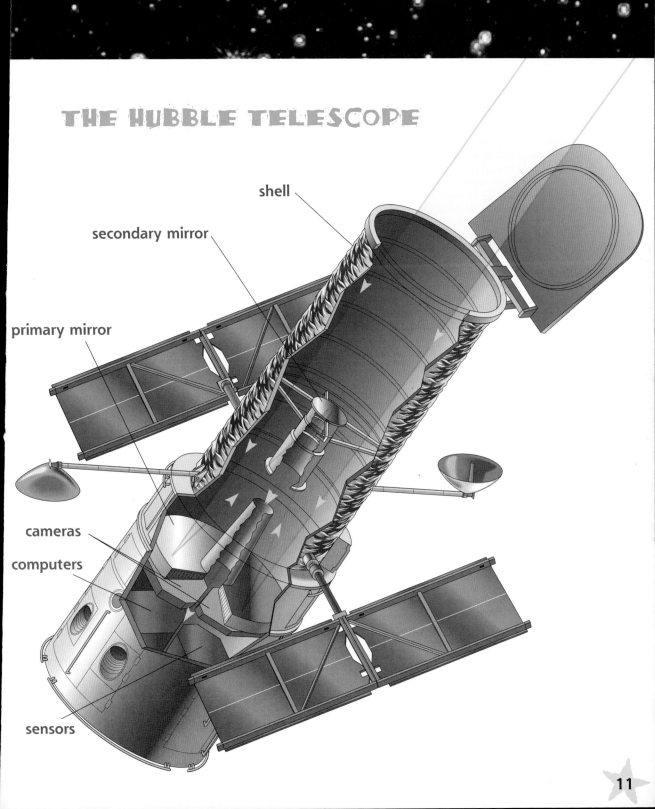

shell

secondary mirror

primary mirror

cameras

computers

sensors

The people who built Hubble had to work in a super-clean environment, free of dust, hairs, and other particles.

12

Despite their extreme care, an error crept into the engineers' calculations. No one knew it yet, but they were off by about two microns—about one-fiftieth the thickness of a human hair. That seemingly tiny error would have a big impact on Hubble's future.

About 10,000 people took part in Hubble's design and construction. Hubble's designers packed it with sensitive instruments that would be able to see things the naked eye cannot.

As the telescope took shape, it began to look like a tin can covered with aluminum foil. That is because Hubble is coated with blankets of Teflon, aluminum, and other protective layers that help keep its temperature steady in space.

The space shuttle carrying the Hubble blasted into space on April 24, 1990.

13

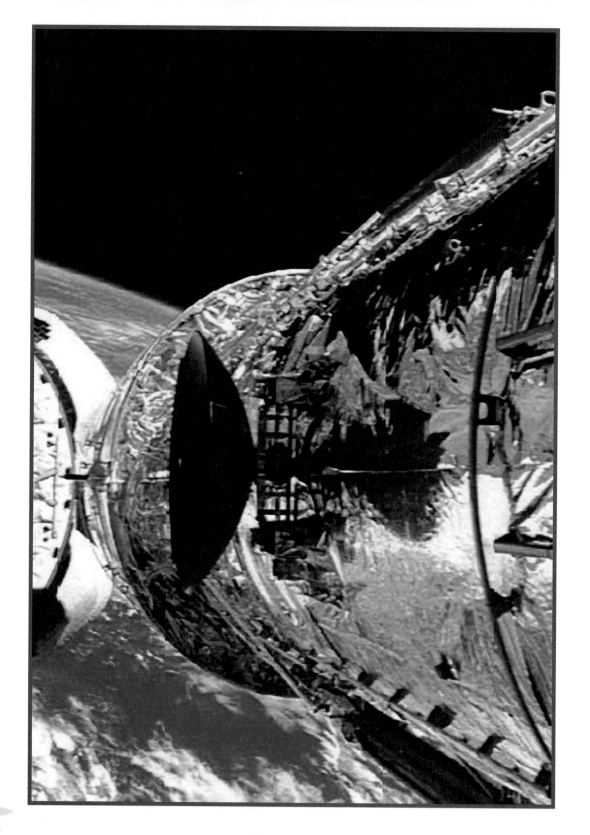

Hubble was supposed to be launched into space in 1983, but technical problems held it up until 1986. Then in 1986, the space shuttle *Challenger* blew up, causing all shuttle flights to be postponed. It wasn't until 1990 that Hubble rode up into orbit on the space shuttle *Discovery*. Scientists all over the world were excited. They believed that decades of work were about to pay off.

The first pictures that Hubble took looked encouraging. But astronomers noticed that they looked fuzzy, and efforts to clear them up failed. Soon it was discovered that the flawed primary mirror was the problem. Hubble could be fixed, but it would take millions of dollars and eat up valuable time. Gloom settled over the entire Hubble project. The gloom would not lift for another three years.

Releasing Hubble from the space shuttle while in orbit was tricky work. One false move could mean a dangerous collision.

When Hubble's problems became public, the telescope became the object of jokes. Newspapers ran headlines like "Pix Nixed as Hubble Sees Double." Comedians poked fun at Hubble's creators for spending $2.2 billion on a nearsighted telescope. But despite the jokes, the situation was serious. Though Hubble still gathered valuable scientific data, Congress threatened to cut off the money for further space research.

There was only one chance to silence the critics. It came on December 2, 1993, when the space shuttle *Endeavour* blasted off on a complex rescue mission. For eleven days, the crew of the *Endeavour* struggled to repair the Hubble. Wearing bulky space suits and battling zero gravity, astronauts made five space walks, a record number, to do repairs. Millions of television viewers tuned in to watch.

★ ★ ★ ★

Astronauts Story Musgrave (right) and Jeffrey A. Hoffman (below) are shown wrapping up work toward the end of their fifth day of space walks.

Endeavour's astronauts had to practice long and hard for this mission. The zero gravity of space cannot be duplicated well here on Earth. So the astronauts practiced by working in water tanks and using virtual reality machines that gave them a sense of weightlessness. Each of the astronauts was trained to do a specific job. But all of them learned how to do one another's jobs as well. That way the mission could go on even if one of the astronauts became ill or was injured.

Once in space, *Endeavour* had to catch Hubble. That was not easy since

★ ★ ★ ★

The conditions in water are similar to the weightlessness of space. Here astronauts Story Musgrave and Jeffrey A. Hoffman practice sliding one of Hubble's cameras into place.

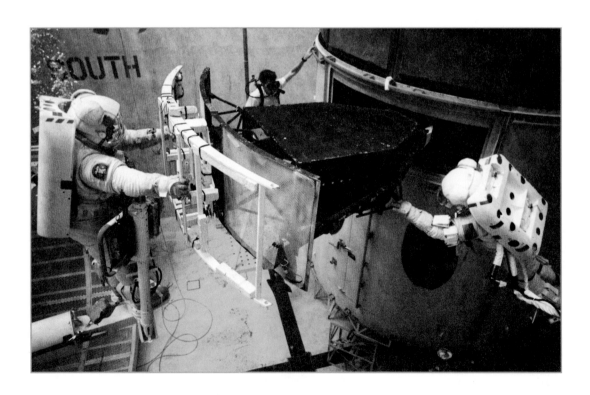

the telescope was whizzing around Earth at 17,500 miles per hour. Once that was accomplished, the astronauts had to bring Hubble into *Endeavour*'s shuttle bay. Hubble's mirror was not the only thing that had to be fixed. The solar panels had become wobbly, making it difficult to point the telescope at one spot and hold it steady. New panels needed to be installed. In all, the astronauts had eleven major repairs or changes to make.

★ ★ ★ ★

The astronauts who fixed Hubble are shown suited up and ready to take off on their historic mission.

★ ★ ★ ★

Hubble's designers equipped it with 76 handholds so that astronauts could move around and do repairs. The idea for the handholds came from astronaut Story Musgrave (shown above). He also became one of the first people to use them.

However, the main problem was still how to fix the primary mirror. It was too difficult to replace, so engineers did the next best thing: They invented a contact lens for Hubble. The contact lens came in the form of a box about the size of a telephone booth. This device took the light coming in from space and refocused it in a way that would allow Hubble to see clearly.

Endeavour's mission went flawlessly. Just over two weeks after the astronauts returned to Earth, scientists gathered to see if the repairs had worked. As the first images appeared, cheers went up. The fuzzy-looking blobs that Hubble had once produced were now crystal-clear images of galaxies and stars. Hubble was fixed, and our view of the universe has not been the same since.

★ ★ ★ ★

Astronaut Kathryn Thornton works with her logbook resting on the arm of her space suit.

HUBBLE SNAPSHOTS

n April 2000, astronomers celebrated the Hubble Space Telescope's tenth anniversary in space. They had good reasons to be happy. By that time, Hubble had zoomed around Earth 58,000 times, studied 13,670 space objects, and produced enough data each day to fill five encyclopedias.

Thanks to this amazing telescope, scientists have an idea of how fast the universe is expanding. Scientists also have a much better idea of how stars and galaxies form and die.

Of all the objects Hubble has photographed, perhaps the most beautiful is a **nebula**—a cloud of gas and dust. All the nebulas on these pages show stars dying in an explosion of light. Over time, the dust and gases they leave behind may reform into new stars and planets.

The Eagle Nebula contains vast columns of gas and dust. The little spikes or knobs sticking out of these columns are bigger than our solar system. The inset photo shows stars forming from a nebula.

Eagle Nebula

Life Cycle of Stars

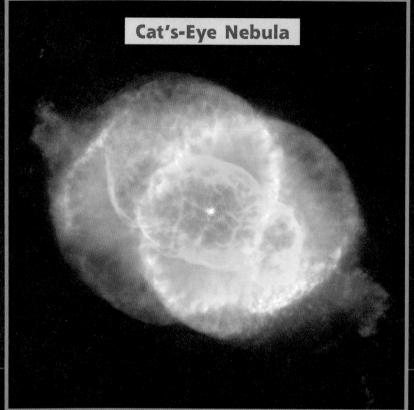

Cat's-Eye Nebula

Special instruments on the Hubble separate light from distant objects into a range of colors, similar to the way a prism separates sunlight. The colors provide astronomers with information such as the age and temperature of an object, as well as what it's made of.

"Twin Jet Nebula"

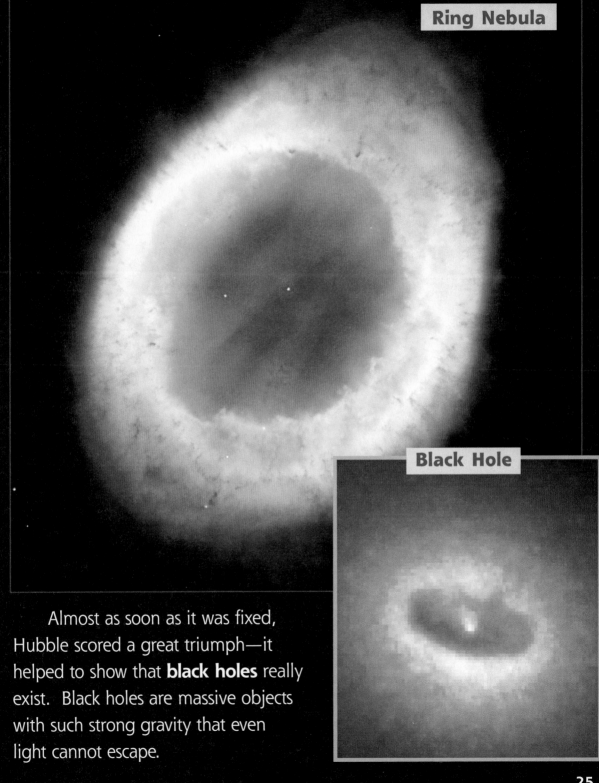

Ring Nebula

Black Hole

Almost as soon as it was fixed, Hubble scored a great triumph—it helped to show that **black holes** really exist. Black holes are massive objects with such strong gravity that even light cannot escape.

Soon after, Hubble took breathtaking photos of a giant comet slamming into Jupiter. Hubble also captured spectacular shots of Saturn and one of the rarest and most spectacular events in space: a **supernova**. A supernova occurs when a giant star explodes, generating more energy in ten seconds than our sun will produce in ten billion years.

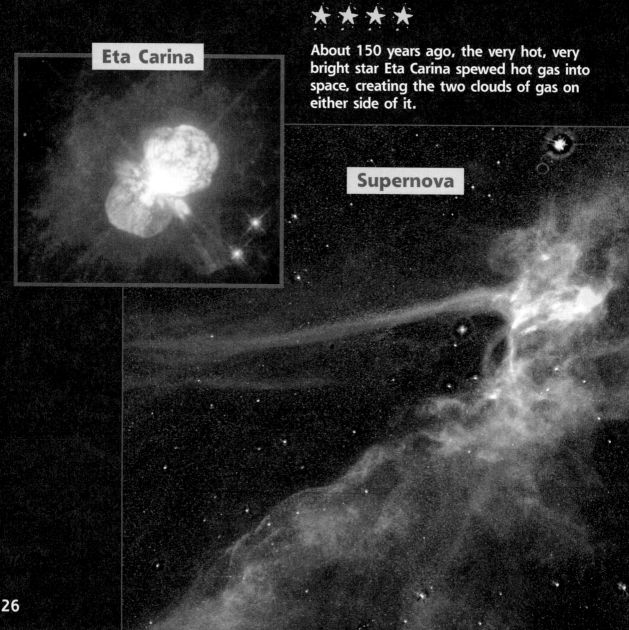

★ ★ ★ ★

About 150 years ago, the very hot, very bright star Eta Carina spewed hot gas into space, creating the two clouds of gas on either side of it.

Eta Carina

Supernova

Jupiter

Saturn

★ ★ ★ ★

In 1994, pieces from the
comet Shoemaker-Levy 9
(shown above) hit Jupiter.
Hubble had an excellent view
of the collision. Each icy chunk
hit the planet with the force of
millions of hydrogen bombs.

Hubble gets maintenance visits from shuttle astronauts every two to three years. In 1997, scientists installed equipment that allowed Hubble to peer even deeper into space. Scientists used the new devices to count the number of observable galaxies. Hubble's improved vision upped their count to over 100 billion galaxies.

Although Hubble's achievements remain impressive, ground-based telescopes are becoming bigger and more powerful all the time. Using computers, they can remove most atmospheric distortions. If the conditions are right, they can get images that are almost as clear as Hubble's.

Hubble's mission will end in 2010. Its replacement, the Next Generation Space Telescope (NGST), is scheduled to arrive in space a year before that. Not only will NGST have a mirror that is ten times larger (and will thus have sharper eyes), it will have better tools for picking up **infrared light**. Infrared is invisible to our eyes, but it helps astronomers spot new planets and study the history of the universe.

★ ★ ★ ★

The Next Generation Space Telescope (NGST) is still on the drawing board. Scientists have come up with several possible designs for it (right and on next page).

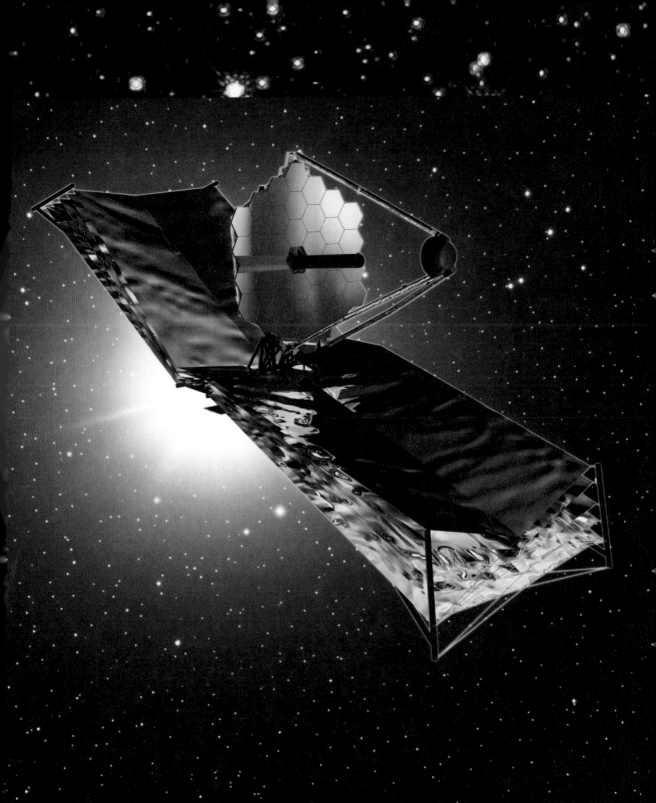

NASA Goddard Space Flight Center

TRW/Ball Aerospace

Astronomers see Hubble and NGST as stepping stones to even bigger achievements. Just as scientists once dreamed of a telescope in orbit, today they dream of a telescope on the moon. From there, they could probe even deeper mysteries in the universe. But such an expensive and ambitious plan is probably decades away. In the meantime, astronomy still owes a big debt to the world's first large space telescope. As one astronomer said of Hubble, "It already has earned a place as one of the wonders of the modern world."

Websites
Check out
http://hubble.stci.edu/discoveries/hstexhibit
http://hubble.gsfc.nasa.gov/
for more information on the Hubble Space Telescope!

GLOSSARY

astronomer: a scientist who studies stars, planets, galaxies, and other objects in space that make up the universe, as well as the universe itself

atmosphere: the layer of gases that surround a planet such as Earth

black hole: an object in space with such strong gravity that even light cannot escape it

galaxy: a huge collection of stars, planets, and space debris that is held together by gravity; some galaxies are spiral, some are oval, others take on more irregular shapes

infrared light: a type of invisible light that lies just beyond red in the spectrum of visible colors

million trillion: 1,000,000,000,000,000,000, or a billion times a billion; also, a million times a million times a million

nebula: a cloud of gas and dust among the stars; nebulas are often the birthplaces of new stars and planets over billions of years

reflecting telescope: a telescope that uses mirrors to focus light

refracting telescope: a telescope that uses lenses to focus light

supernova: the bright, powerful explosion that occurs when a massive star dies

ultraviolet light: a type of invisible light that lies just beyond violet in the spectrum of visible colors

universe: all the stars, planets, galaxies, matter, space, and energy known to exist

INDEX